THE TUSKEGEE AIRMEN

THE TUSKEGEE AIRMEN

ESSENTIAL LIBRARY OF
WORLD WAR II

Essential Library

An Imprint of Abdo Publishing
abdopublishing.com

BY CHRISTINE ZUCHORA-WALSKE

CONTENT CONSULTANT

ALLISON J. GOUGH, PHD
CHAIR, DEPARTMENT OF HISTORY
HAWAI'I PACIFIC UNIVERSITY

abdopublishing.com

Published by Abdo Publishing, a division of ABDO, PO Box 398166, Minneapolis, Minnesota 55439. Copyright © 2016 by Abdo Consulting Group, Inc. International copyrights reserved in all countries. No part of this book may be reproduced in any form without written permission from the publisher. Essential Library™ is a trademark and logo of Abdo Publishing.

Printed in the United States of America, North Mankato, Minnesota

052015
092015

 THIS BOOK CONTAINS
RECYCLED MATERIALS

Cover Photo: US Army Signal Corps/AP Images
Interior Photos: US Army Signal Corps/AP Images, 1, 3; US Air Force, 6, 9, 11, 12, 13, 15, 33, 34, 37, 39, 44, 46, 48, 50, 55, 56, 62, 68, 70, 72, 75, 80, 91, 93, 95, 98 (bottom); North Wind Picture Archives, 16; Library of Congress, 20, 22, 29, 52, 67, 98 (top); Everett Collection, 25; MPI/Getty Images, 26; US National Archives and Records Administration, 32, 99 (top); Mondadori Portfolio/Getty Images, 41; AP Images, 58, 65; Red Line Editorial, 61; Ralph Morse/The LIFE Images Collection/Getty Images, 77; Bettmann/Corbis, 82, 99 (bottom); Matt York/AP Images, 88; Afro American Newspapers/Gado/Getty Images, 85; Jim Steinfeldt/Michael Ochs Archives/Getty Images, 86; Dave Martin/AP Images, 96

Editor: Arnold Ringstad
Series Designers: Kelsey Oseid and Maggie Villaume

Library of Congress Control Number: 2015931120
Cataloging-in-Publication Data

Zuchora-Walske, Christine.
  The Tuskegee airmen / Christine Zuchora-Walske.
   p. cm. -- (Essential library of World War II)
  Includes bibliographical references and index.
  ISBN 978-1-62403-795-5
  1. United States. Army Air Forces. Fighter Group, 332nd--Juvenile literature. 2. United States. Army Air Forces. Fighter Squadron, 99th--Juvenile literature. 3. United States. Army Air Forces. Fighter Group, 477th--Juvenile literature. 4. World War, 1939-1945--Aerial operations, American--Juvenile literature. 5. World War, 1939-1945--Participation, African American--Juvenile literature.
  I. Title.
  940.54--dc23

2015931120

CONTENTS

B-24s and other US heavy bombers flew in large formations over enemy targets.

RED-TAIL ANGELS

Jim Scheib was a 20-year-old from Pittsburgh, Pennsylvania, deployed to combat in World War II in October 1944. He was assigned as copilot of a B-24 bomber aircraft as part of the 485th Bombardment Group based in Venosa, Italy. The US military was segregated at this time, with white and African-American soldiers split into separate units. The 485th was all-white.

It was not long before the bomber, named *Tail Heavy*, and its crew of ten men were flying missions over German-occupied Europe. Their job was to weaken Germany's ability to continue the war by destroying transportation infrastructure and oil refineries behind enemy lines.

TAIL HEAVY IN TROUBLE

On November 17, 1944, *Tail Heavy* and 27 other B-24 bombers flew a mission deep into Germany. They were accompanied, as usual, by an escort of fighter planes. Each bomber had ten machine guns for defense, but experience had shown the large, lumbering bombers were not agile enough to protect themselves effectively from enemy fighters. During this mission, antiaircraft fire from the ground hit Scheib's bomber, puncturing the oxygen tanks that supplied breathable air to four of the ten crew members. The bombers were flying in formation at an altitude of 25,000 feet (7,620 m), where the atmosphere was too thin to sustain the men. Without oxygen, the four crew members, including the pilot, soon passed out. It would be only a matter of minutes before the men would suffer permanent brain damage and, eventually, death.

Luckily for copilot Scheib, his oxygen supply was still working. He was in charge now, and he had to think fast. What should he do? If he stayed in formation, the other bombers and their machine guns would protect his crippled plane and its crew from German fighters. But he thought to himself, "If I stay here, I'll take four dead guys back with me."[1] For Scheib, that was an unacceptable option.

The other possibility was to fly back to base at a much lower altitude. Lower down, oxygen masks were unnecessary. But flying alone at a low altitude was very dangerous. German fighters would easily spot *Tail Heavy* and see it was a straggler with no escort. The Germans were known for attacking stragglers. Scheib could revive his crew mates by flying lower, but they might all pay a steep price for it if German fighters found them.

Scheib decided the risk was worth it. He could not let his four comrades die. He had to at least give them a chance. So he waggled his plane's tail to let the

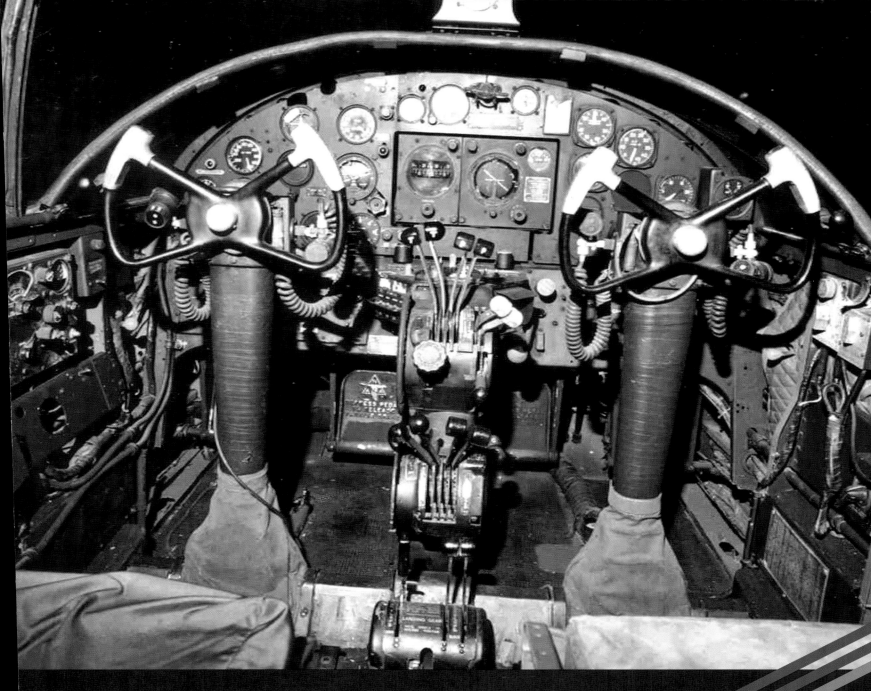

Sitting in the cramped cockpit beside the passed-out pilot, Scheib needed to think quickly to save his fellow airmen.

other bomber crews know he was leaving formation. Then he steered *Tail Heavy* into a steep dive.

Ten thousand feet (3,048 m) lower, Scheib leveled out. At 15,000 feet (4,572 m), the air was rich with oxygen, and his crew mates regained consciousness. Scheib told all the men to put on their parachutes and be ready to bail out if German fighters pounced on them.

Scheib was on the lookout for German planes, but what he saw next was something he did not expect. *Tail Heavy*'s flight engineer tapped him on the shoulder and pointed. Scheib looked out the window and saw a P-51 Mustang. The US fighter airplane had a tail painted bright red. It was one of the Tuskegee Airmen—known to other fliers as Red Tails. The Tuskegee Airmen were an all-African-American unit of fighter pilots. They had a reputation for protecting US bombers in the skies over Europe. "Where did this guy come from?" Scheib wondered.[2]

The Red Tail had seen Scheib leaving formation and had followed him. Soon another fighter showed up on his other wing. A wave of relief washed over Scheib. He knew he and his crew had a much better chance of surviving this flight now. The presence of these two fighters announced to anyone watching that an entire escort squadron of fighter planes was nearby. He felt nobody would dare mess with *Tail Heavy* knowing that.

Scheib was right. His plane made it back to Venosa safely, thanks in large part to its Red Tail escort. But that was not the last time he would encounter the Red Tails.

THE P-51 MUSTANG

From 1944 through the end of World War II, the primary aircraft flown by Tuskegee Airmen in the 332nd Fighter Group was the P-51 Mustang. Experts on both sides of the conflict agreed the P-51 was among the best fighter airplanes of the war. The first model of the aircraft, known as the P-51A, entered service with the US military in March 1942. However, the airplane's engine lacked power at high altitudes. In late 1942, the military experimented with replacing the Mustang's existing engine with a Merlin engine manufactured by the British company Rolls-Royce.

A member of the Tuskegee Airmen ground crew loads ammunition into a Mustang's wing machine gun.

The new engine boosted the Mustang's power immensely. This new model, the P-51B, could fly faster and higher, speeding across the sky at nearly 440 miles per hour (710 kmh). Later changes made the plane even more effective. The P-51D added a transparent plastic bubble canopy, or cockpit enclosure, allowing the pilot to see clearly in all directions. This was an improvement over earlier canopies, which had braces that blocked a pilot's rear vision.

The P-51 carried four to six machine guns and could also carry bombs and rockets. Its extra external fuel tanks gave it a range of more than 1,000 miles (1,609 km).[3] Hermann Göring, the commander of Germany's Luftwaffe, or air force, remarked after the war, "When I saw your bombers over Berlin protected by your long-range fighters [P-51 Mustangs], I knew then that the Luftwaffe would be unable to stop your bombers. Our weapons plants would be destroyed; our defeat was inevitable."[4]

AN UNEXPECTEDLY HAPPY NEW YEAR

Exactly six weeks later, the 485th flew a mission to bomb an enemy railroad facility in northern Italy. On their way back to base, they learned their home runway was snowed in. The bombers could not land on a snowy steel runway, so they had to land elsewhere.

The place chosen for them was Ramitelli, home base of the 332nd Fighter Group—the Red Tails. Ramitelli was an all-black base. African-American soldiers and white soldiers did not live or work together on equal footing. Housing the 485th at Ramitelli created an unprecedented racially integrated situation. There was no telling what might happen.

As it turned out, the stay was warm and festive. The men of the 332nd shared their tents, blankets, rations, and Christmas cookies from home. The men of the 485th gratefully accepted the Red Tails' hospitality. Men from both groups shared their stories, and a bond was forged among them. If any airman was upset about the situation, he kept it to himself.

HIDDEN HATRED

Lieutenant Louis Purnell of the 332nd Fighter Group was responsible for censoring all mail that left Ramitelli Airfield. Censoring mail was routine during World War II. Censors read the mail and blacked out any information the enemy might find useful.

During the 485th's stay at Ramitelli, Purnell's duties included censoring the white men's letters. In one letter, Purnell read complaints from a gunner of the 485th who used derogatory language about being forced to live, sleep, and eat with African-American airmen.

Purnell did not want to upset what was otherwise a peaceful situation, so he said nothing. But the letter reminded him racist hate could still burn beneath an appearance of friendship and calm.

Due to the segregation of the US military, Ramitelli had been set aside as an African-American base.

As they rang in the new year together, the airmen of the 485th and the Red Tails at Ramitelli showed what could happen when African Americans and white Americans met as equals. But this sort of experience, unfortunately, was unusual for African Americans. In fact, it had been a long, hard battle for the Tuskegee Airmen simply to gain the right to serve their country in combat.

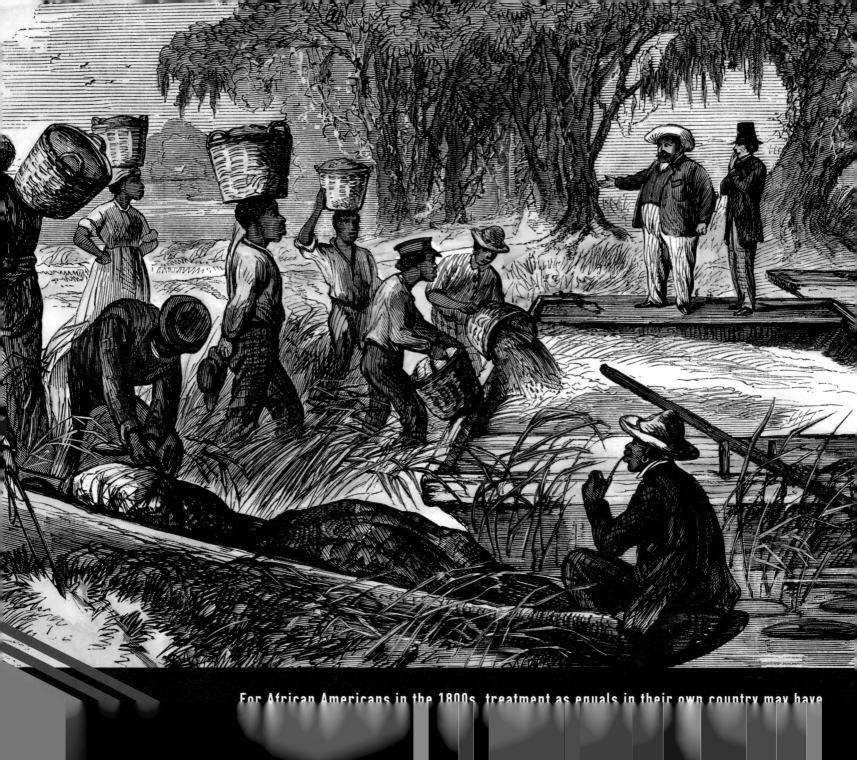

For African Americans in the 1800s, treatment as equals in their own country may have

THE LONG ROAD TO TAKEOFF

By the 1940s, people of African ancestry had been living in North America for more than three centuries. Until 1865, slavery was legal in the United States, and most African Americans were slaves. Slave owners considered them property.

Although free African Americans had it a little better than slaves during the US slave era, life was still difficult. Free African Americans owned their own labor, but their employment opportunities were limited, and their treatment by white society was poor. This was true both in slave states and in states that had abolished slavery.

Conditions worsened for free African Americans over time. Before approximately 1800, free black men had some civil rights. In some parts of the United States, for example, they could work in

SLAVERY IN THE UNITED STATES

Slave owners housed and fed their slaves but did not pay slaves for their work. Owners controlled every aspect of their slaves' lives. And for most slaves, life was very hard. They typically lived in crowded, poorly built cabins. They ate a monotonous diet, often consisting of salt pork, molasses, corn bread, and little else. Slaves often worked as field hands on plantations, performing backbreaking labor from sunup to sundown as soon as they were big enough—usually around age ten. Slaves had no civil rights. They could not own anything. Whatever items they kept in their cabins, wore on their bodies, or otherwise used belonged to their owners. Slaves could not leave their owners' property without permission, could not vote or testify in court, and were forbidden to learn how to read or write. They could be sold away and separated from their families at any time. They were often punished for infractions such as not working hard enough, being late, running away, and defying authority. Punishments included severe measures such as imprisonment, mutilation, torture, and whipping.

skilled trades, vote, and serve on juries. But after 1800, things changed. One key factor was the 1793 invention of Eli Whitney's cotton gin. This device sped up the processing of cotton, making it lucrative for Southern farmers to grow large cotton crops. These crops required large amounts of slave labor to be profitable.

As slavery in the South expanded, white Americans increasingly felt the need to justify slavery. They did so by spreading racist ideas. They described the many ways in which they believed African Americans were inferior to white Americans. Some even suggested African Americans were better off as slaves. As a result, during the early and mid-1800s, free blacks slowly and steadily lost what few rights they had. They endured more violence and intimidation. In 1857, the US Supreme Court ruled in *Dred Scott v. Sanford* that no African Americans, slave or free, were citizens or could ever become citizens. Without citizenship, they had little hope of improving their standing in society.

CIVIL WAR

Throughout the early and mid-1800s, as the cotton economy took over the South and slavery expanded, an American antislavery movement called abolitionism gathered strength. Some abolitionists wanted to return African-American slaves to Africa. They raised money to buy slaves' freedom, establish the nation of Liberia in West Africa, and transport freed slaves there. Other abolitionists, including most African Americans, opposed this idea. They saw US slavery as a moral outrage that needed to end immediately. They pointed to the Declaration of Independence, which states "all men are created equal, that they are endowed by their Creator with certain unalienable Rights, that among these are Life, Liberty and the pursuit of Happiness."[1] They said the United States should be a haven of freedom for all humankind. They called for freeing all

JUSTIFYING SLAVERY

In 1850, Virginia lawyer George Fitzhugh published an essay titled "The Universal Law of Slavery." Demonstrating racism that was common for his era, he describes why he believes African Americans must be kept as slaves for their own good:

> He the Negro is but a grown up child, and must be governed as a child. . . . The master occupies toward him the place of parent or guardian.

> The negro is improvident. . . . He would become an insufferable burden to society. Society has the right to prevent this, and can only do so by subjecting him to domestic slavery. . . .

> The negro slaves of the South are the happiest, and, in some sense, the freest people in the world. . . . 'Tis happiness in itself—and results from contentment with the present, and confident assurance of the future.[2]

slaves and having African Americans join US society as citizens. These abolitionists were persistent. They published and distributed literature to support their position. They sent petitions to state officials and to the US Congress. They ran for public office, campaigning on abolitionist principles.

By 1860, abolitionists had gained a strong foothold in the Republican Party. In that year's November elections, Republicans ran on an antislavery platform, and Americans elected Republican Abraham Lincoln as president. Southerners were shocked and angry. They believed the Union no longer had a place for them. Within three months, seven Southern states seceded from the United States and formed the Confederate States of America. In his March 1861 inaugural address, Lincoln announced he did not intend to end slavery but

Though Lincoln did not originally set out to end slavery, the Civil War achieved this goal.

that it was his duty to preserve the Union. This statement displeased many Southerners. In April 1861, Confederate forces attacked a US fort in South Carolina, and the US Civil War (1861–1865) began.

Four years and more than 600,000 deaths later, the Civil War ended and Reconstruction, the process of rebuilding US society, began. It would continue through 1877. The Thirteenth, Fourteenth, and Fifteenth Amendments to the US Constitution abolished slavery, granted citizenship to all people born in the United States, and guaranteed no male citizen would be denied the right to vote based on race. For several years, conditions for blacks living in the South improved. Many African-American men voted, and approximately 600 held public office at the local, state, and federal levels through the 1870s.[3] Public spaces, such as trains and restaurants, began to integrate racially. African Americans could now own land.

Many white Southerners found this new situation intolerable. Established white leaders were no longer in power. The Southern economy struggled to find its way without slavery. And perhaps most important, many whites could not accept a society in which blacks and whites were equals. Fear and hatred grew. Amid this climate, armed white supremacist groups such as the Ku Klux Klan (KKK) formed. With violence and intimidation, whites steadily deprived African Americans of their voting rights, regained control of public offices, and passed laws that enforced segregation. This system of laws, rules, and customs, which operated mainly in the American South from 1887 to the 1960s, came to be known as Jim Crow.

Segregation under Jim Crow even dictated which drinking fountains or public restrooms

Although Jim Crow primarily affected the South, segregation existed in the North, too. In the South, segregation was part of the region's laws. In the North, it was often a matter of practical reality. African Americans lived in separate neighborhoods, partly because they wanted to stick together and partly because these neighborhoods were the ones African Americans could afford with the low-paying jobs they could get. In addition, landlords and realtors steered African Americans away from white neighborhoods. Meanwhile, city ordinances and homeowners' agreements, upheld by judges, accomplished the same result.

By the end of the 1800s, this type of racial segregation had the blessing of the federal government. In 1896, the US Supreme Court ruled on the case of *Plessy v. Ferguson*. It said "separate but equal" facilities for whites and African Americans were acceptable under the Fourteenth Amendment. This decision affirmed the widespread belief among white Americans that darker-skinned people were less intelligent and less civilized than lighter-skinned people.

JIM CROW TIMELINE

1838	White actor Thomas Dartmouth Rice, performing in blackface as a character named Jim Crow, popularizes the name as a slang term meaning "African American."
1875	Congress passes the Civil Rights Act of 1875, which outlaws racial discrimination in public facilities.
1877	Withdrawal of federal troops from the South ends Reconstruction.
1882–1951	A total of 3,438 African Americans are recorded to have been lynched. The true figure is likely much higher.
1883	The US Supreme Court rules that the Civil Rights Act of 1875 is unconstitutional.
1890–1908	Southern states pass laws intended to prevent African Americans from voting.
1896	*Plessy v. Ferguson* establishes the "separate but equal" principle.

1913–1921	President Woodrow Wilson segregates government employees.
1914	All Southern states and many Northern cities have segregation laws.
1915	The movie *Birth of a Nation* promotes the KKK and racial stereotypes about African Americans.
1915–1930	Up to 1 million African Americans move from the rural South to Southern cities, Northern cities, and the West in the Great Migration.
1917	Ten thousand African Americans march silently down New York City's Fifth Avenue to protest racial oppression.
1919	During Red Summer, resentful whites riot against African-American efforts to gain equality.
1920–1925	The KKK peaks in size at approximately 3 million members.[4]

African Americans have served in their country's military for hundreds of years.

AFRICAN AMERICANS IN THE MILITARY

Harsh discrimination kept most African Americans out of military service through World War II. However, throughout US history there were always African Americans who were determined to serve their country and their ideals despite the poor treatment they received in return.

In the 1600s, some North American colonies either required African Americans to assist in the colonies' defense or permitted them to enlist in militias. The military status of African Americans varied among the colonies, but generally speaking, free blacks were welcome in the military while slaves were not welcome. Many white colonists did not want to arm and train slaves for fear of enabling them to revolt against their masters. These rules and customs were often suspended in times of emergency, when all able-bodied men were needed for defense.

At the outset of the Revolutionary War (1775–1783) in July 1775, the Continental army banned African Americans from joining. Then the Americans learned of an offer made by the British governor of Virginia in November, inviting free African Americans to join the fight on the side of the British. By December 1775, the Continental army changed its policy to welcome free African Americans. Slaves were still banned, but some participated anyway as substitutes for their masters. By the end of the war, approximately 5,000 African Americans had served in the Continental army, and they participated in most major battles.[1] The Continental navy, frequently short on men, never banned African Americans. Many African Americans were skilled sailors, and the navy could not afford to turn them away.

African Americans who served in the Revolutionary War benefited from their service. Some who were slaves received freedom, and others got land grants from the government. But overall, US society forgot the contributions of African Americans to US independence from Great Britain. Similarly, white Americans ignored the skill, bravery, and leadership of African American soldiers and sailors who fought in the War of 1812 (1812–1815) between the United States and Great Britain and the Seminole Wars (1817–1858) between the United States and the Seminoles, a group of Native Americans who lived in Florida.

THE CIVIL WAR

When the Civil War began in April 1861, African Americans immediately volunteered for Union military service. But President Lincoln insisted the

Huge numbers of African-American soldiers fought for the Union during the Civil War.

war's goal was to preserve the Union, not free slaves. He feared enlisting African-American soldiers would send the wrong message and would drive the slavery-permitting states that remained in the Union to join the Confederacy. In addition, he did not expect the war to last more than a few months, so he did not expect to need huge numbers of troops. The US War Department announced, "This Department . . . has no intention at present to call into the service of the Government any colored soldiers."[2] Furthermore, many government leaders believed African Americans were either incapable of fighting effectively or would simply refuse to do so.

But as the war dragged on, Union volunteer recruitment dropped, and Union leaders watched with dismay as the Confederacy put African Americans to work for its cause. By the end of 1861, Union forces began using African-American workers in military support roles. By mid-1862, the War Department was accepting African-American volunteers. Lincoln issued the Emancipation Proclamation on January 1, 1863, freeing all slaves within the Confederacy. The proclamation made it clear the abolition of slavery was a key war goal, and African Americans flocked to fight for the Union. By the end of the Civil War, nearly 200,000 black soldiers and sailors had fought for the Union army and navy in racially segregated units.[3]

The custom of racial segregation in US military units that began during the Civil War became official policy in 1869. This policy stayed in place through the first half of the 1900s. The general belief among military and civilian authorities, as well as in society at large, said African Americans lacked the intelligence for combat. Most black soldiers were assigned to manual labor units. The few assigned to combat in racially segregated units received poor training, equipment, and leadership—and as a result, they often performed poorly, unfairly reinforcing stereotypes about their abilities.

WORLD WAR I

More than 400,000 African Americans served in the US military during World War I (1914–1918), 90 percent of them in labor units and 10 percent in combat.[4] They performed admirably, but they received little or no reward in the United States for their efforts. However, the French government gave prestigious military awards to African-American fighters who fought in that country.

Pioneering African-American pilot Eugene Jacques Bullard fought in France both on the ground and in the air. From 1912 to 1914, Bullard worked as a vaudeville performer and a boxer, traveling all around western Europe. When World War I began, he joined the French army's 170th Infantry Regiment. The members of this famous regiment were known as the Swallows of Death; Bullard became known as the Black Swallow of Death. He fought bravely and was wounded twice at the 1916 Battle of Verdun, for which he earned a slew of French military decorations.

After recovering from his wounds, Bullard wanted to return to combat but was declared unfit for infantry duty. He requested flight training with the French air force—an assignment typically forbidden to African Americans in the US military—and received it. He went on to become the first-ever African-American military pilot. He flew many combat missions with the French air force and shot down at least one German plane.[5] Bullard settled in Paris after the war.

Many black veterans returned home to communities resentful of their service. In New Orleans, Louisiana, a white speaker told them, "You . . . were wondering

AVIATION IN WORLD WAR I

The American inventors the Wright Brothers had invented the airplane in 1903, more than a decade before World War I broke out. When the war began, it soon became clear this recent invention would play an important role in warfare. Early in the war, airplanes were largely used as reconnaissance platforms. Pilots could survey the battlefield from high above. Eventually, pilots began firing at enemy pilots using pistols or rifles. In 1915, the war's second year, machine guns were fitted to aircraft. The fighter plane, equipped to destroy enemy aircraft, was born.

African-American troops served in France during World War I.

how you are going to be treated after the war. Well, I'll tell you, you are going to be treated exactly like you were before the war; this is a white man's country and we expect to rule it."[6] In some areas, whites attacked African-American veterans who came home from war, then blamed the veterans for the violence. Meanwhile, white officers in the military circulated reports about African-American cowardice and poor leadership qualities. By the 1930s, this discrimination led the military to strictly limit African-American participation in the US armed forces.

EUGENE JACQUES BULLARD

1895–1961

Eugene Jacques Bullard was born in Columbus, Georgia, on October 9, 1895. His father, William, had been born into slavery on a cotton plantation. His mother, Josephine, had Creek Indian ancestry. In 1901, Eugene began attending school, where he learned to read. During this time, his father narrowly escaped being lynched. Shaken by this incident, Eugene ran away from home—and away from Columbus—in 1906. He went on to serve in France during World War I, settling there after the war's end.

When Nazi Germany invaded and occupied France in 1940, Bullard escaped by bicycling to Portugal. There he found passage to New York City on a Red Cross ship. Soon thereafter, Bullard arranged for the rescue of his daughters. His wife, however, refused to leave France. Eventually the two divorced.

Bullard spent the rest of his life in New York. He worked at a variety of jobs and lived in relative obscurity. In 1959, the French government made him a Knight of the Legion of Honor. Membership in the Legion of Honor is the highest decoration in France. Bullard died in 1961, still unnoticed by his fellow Americans or the US government. It was not until 1994 that the US Air Force posthumously gave him an officer's commission as lieutenant.

The Tuskegee Airmen underwent intensive training before being sent to the front lines.

FLIGHT TRAINING AT TUSKEGEE

For African Americans, the experience of World War I and its aftermath had been very disappointing. They had believed their military service would encourage white Americans to see them as fellow citizens who deserved full civil rights. Instead, white society had twisted the truth and used it to strengthen racist ideas and racial discrimination.

In 1937, the US Army War College reaffirmed its 1925 study "Employment of Negro Man Power in War." This report claims African Americans had smaller brains and were inherently cowardly. Thus, the War College said, African-American military participation should remain limited in size and scope. The percentage of blacks in the military, it said, should reflect the percentage of African Americans in the US population. And African

Americans would only be allowed to serve in low-skill jobs such as cleaning, cooking, and carrying.

But by the late 1930s, this policy was becoming hard for US military leaders to justify from a perspective of sheer manpower. While the United States was turning away qualified military recruits simply because of their skin color, the rest of the world was sliding steadily toward war.

A GATHERING STORM

In 1933, Adolf Hitler and his Nazi political party rose to power in Germany. Germany under the Nazis wanted to take over Europe and increase its territory while purging that space of ethnic groups the Nazis deemed undesirable. Among the many undesirable groups they identified, the Nazis especially hated Jews. They also believed people of African descent were inferior to whites.

THE WAR COLLEGE REPORT

The War College's 1925 report describes the supposed attributes of African Americans in great detail. Its unscientific and racist assumptions are obvious as such today, but were taken seriously decades ago. They include the following passages:

1. The Negro is physically qualified for combat duty. He is by nature subservient and believes himself to be inferior to the white man. He is most susceptible to the influence of crowd psychology. He can not control himself in the fear of danger to the extent the white man can. He has not the initiative and resourcefulness of the white man. He is mentally inferior to the white man.

2. In past wars the negro has made a fair laborer. As a technician and fighter he has been inferior to the white man.

3. In the World War the negro officer was a failure in combat.[1]

Germany's skilled pilots played a major role in the early Nazi successes during the war.

In pursuit of its goals, Germany invaded its eastern neighbor, Poland, in September 1939. Poland's allies, the United Kingdom and France, then declared war on Germany. The war, which eventually came to be called World War II, quickly spread throughout Europe and drew in many other nations. Germany, Italy, and Japan, collectively called the Axis powers, fought on one side. On the other side fought a group of nations known as the Allies, whose key members were the United Kingdom, France, the Soviet Union, the United States, and China. The United States would not enter the war immediately, however, hoping the conflict would remain a principally European problem.

Beginning in 1939, one European nation after another—including Poland, France, Denmark, Norway, Luxembourg, the Netherlands, and Belgium—fell to Germany. Japan already occupied a large chunk of China and was eyeing the US-held Pacific islands of the Philippines, Guam, and Hawaii. The United States prepared to defend itself by building up its troops, training, and equipment. Most leaders believed airpower would be crucial, so they put effort into creating a modern air force, then called the Army Air Corps.

In 1940, the United States began drafting men into military service. US military policy specifically forbade African Americans from serving alongside white troops. It also excluded blacks from the Army Air Corps. African Americans could not be military pilots because pilots were officers. According to Major General Henry Arnold, chief of the Army Air Corps, "having Negro officers serving over white enlisted men . . . would create an impossible social problem."[2]

THE CIVILIAN PILOT TRAINING PROGRAM

General Arnold's proclamation may have discouraged some African Americans who wanted to fly, but it did not change the United States' desperate need for pilots. The Army Air Corps planned to mobilize tens of thousands of airplanes, and it was starting out with fewer than 5,000 pilots.[3] The United States needed to train thousands of pilots as quickly as possible.

To achieve this ambitious goal, leaders turned to the Civilian Pilot Training Program (CPTP). The government had created this program through an act of

The CPTP provided flight training for many new pilots, including women.

Congress in 1939. Its stated purpose was to boost the US aviation industry—but its true purpose was to provide a pool of pilots from which the military could draw if necessary. During the legislative process, Illinois representative Everett Dirksen had added language stating that "none of the benefits of training or programs shall be denied on account of race, creed, or color."[4] Dirksen had been impressed by the accomplishments and arguments of two African-American airmen, John Robinson and Cornelius Coffey, who promoted the inclusion of African Americans in the CPTP.

After heated debate, the bill passed in August 1939 with Dirksen's language. Shortly thereafter, President Franklin D. Roosevelt signed the bill into law. The CPTP would eventually make it possible for the Tuskegee Airmen to take flight.

THE CPTP AT TUSKEGEE

Under the CPTP, the federal government provided funding to 1,132 US colleges and universities so they could recruit aviation students, hold piloting classes, and conduct flight training for students who passed the classes.[5] The standards for passing were very high. This was designed to weed out marginal pilots whose failings would be deadly in a real flight.

Thanks to the antidiscrimination language in the law authorizing the CPTP, the government could not reject qualified applications from historically African-American colleges simply on the basis of race. As a result, the participating schools included six such colleges. The first and most prominent of these six colleges was the Tuskegee Institute in Tuskegee, Alabama.

The Tuskegee Institute started its first CPTP class in December 1939 with 20 students. In March 1940, the 19 remaining students in that class took their civilian pilot licensing exam.[6] All of them passed on the first try. They were just the first group of African-American aviators to pass through the Tuskegee program. Many more followed after them. The CPTP at Tuskegee and other African-American schools quickly increased the number of African-American licensed civilian pilots.

JOHN ROBINSON
1903–1954

John Robinson was not a Tuskegee Airman. But it is likely that without his efforts, there would have been no Tuskegee Airmen at all. Robinson was born in 1903 in Carrabella, Florida. As a young man, he noticed that automobiles were growing more and more important. He worked hard to pay tuition at Tuskegee Institute so he could become an auto mechanic. He graduated in 1924 and moved north to Detroit, Michigan, the auto-manufacturing capital of the United States.

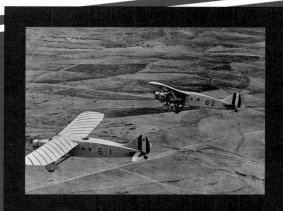

Italian aircraft threatened the skies over Ethiopia, prompting pilots such as Robinson to assist the African nation.

He later applied to the Curtiss Wright Aeronautical Institute in Chicago, Illinois. The school accepted him, and he paid his tuition and enrolled. But when he showed up on the first day of class in 1929 and the staff discovered he was African American, they turned him away. Robinson and his friend Cornelius Coffey, another black enrollee, threatened to sue the school, which then reluctantly admitted them. Both graduated in 1931.

In 1934, Robinson flew with Coffey from Chicago to Tuskegee so they could try to persuade the institute's administrators to begin teaching flying there. Meanwhile, the leader of Ethiopia also invited Robinson to lead the nation's fledgling air force against an invasion by Italy. Robinson accepted Ethiopia's offer, and he earned his nickname the Brown Condor in combat over Africa. Although Italy won the conflict, Robinson returned to the United States a hero.

A NEW FIGHTER SQUADRON

African-American pilots who wanted to serve in the US military—even those who completed CPTP training—still faced a big obstacle in 1940. The draft that began in late summer of that year forbade African-American pilots in the Army Air Corps. However, things were about to change. President Roosevelt was running for another term in the upcoming election of November 1940. His opponent was campaigning on an antiracism platform, pledging to desegregate the US military. Because of this, Roosevelt feared losing the support of African-American voters and their white allies. To appeal to these voters, Roosevelt pressured his secretary of war, Henry Stimson, to open the Army Air Corps to African-American aviators. Although Stimson was personally opposed to this plan, he had to follow the president's orders. In October 1940, the government, heavily lobbied by civil rights leaders, announced African Americans would be accepted as pilots and mechanics in the US military.

TUSKEGEE UNIVERSITY

On July 4, 1881, the state of Alabama established the Tuskegee Normal School for Colored Teachers. A normal school is designed to train new teachers. It began with 30 students in a room at a local church, taught by the school's first president and teacher, Booker T. Washington.[7] The school soon moved to a nearby abandoned plantation, where the center of the campus remains. Under Washington, the school grew in size and importance and became a leader in industrial education, changing its name to the Tuskegee Normal and Industrial Institute. In 1896, George Washington Carver joined Tuskegee and made many important agricultural advances. In the 1930s and 1940s, Tuskegee became the center of African-American military aviation. In the 1950s and 1960s, it was deeply involved in the US civil rights movement. In 1985, it changed its name to Tuskegee University.

The Army Air Corps was not, however, required to integrate racially. So it began planning a separate African-American flying unit. In January 1941, the War Department announced the Army Air Corps would create an all-African-American fighter squadron. This announcement met with mixed reactions.

The majority of white Americans still believed blacks were inferior and should stay in subordinate roles. They had a hard time accepting African Americans could fly military planes. Whites had assumed if blacks could even fly, they would have to fly cargo planes, performing the customary African-American role as support troops rather than combat troops. But in the Army Air Corps' plan, African Americans would fly fighters. Fighter pilots were the military's most glamorous soldiers, because their job was so demanding and deadly.

Ironically, it was racism that brought about the decision. African Americans could not fly cargo planes because transport units constantly interacted with other units. Black officers flying cargo planes would often encounter white enlisted men in other units. The authorities believed these encounters would create the "impossible social problem" of African-American men having authority over white men that General Arnold had warned against.[8] A fighter squadron was more isolated. It could train at its own airfield. Once deployed into combat, it could fly missions from its own base. With this plan, the military could stay segregated. It could avoid upsetting the traditional model of white authority over African Americans. This, at least, was a principle most whites supported.

African Americans, for their part, reacted to the Army Air Corps' announcement with a mixture of satisfaction and disappointment. A separate

The Tuskegee Airmen's use of fighter planes made them an independent fighting force, helping ensure they would remain segregated from white military units.

African-American air force was humiliating; it suggested African-American aviators did not measure up to white aviators. And it was depressing that the military, which already had ample pilot-training facilities, would waste the time, money, and effort to establish a self-contained African-American pilots' training base. This showed how illogical American racism was. But African-American leaders were practical, too. They realized the creation of African-American flying units was a vital step on the road to a bigger goal: integrating the Army Air Corps. After that, perhaps someday the entire US military could be integrated.

TUSKEGEE ARMY AIR FIELD

In March 1941, the Army Air Corps officially created the Ninety-Ninth Pursuit Squadron and soon thereafter began building the Tuskegee Army Air Field (TAAF), the squadron's training base, near the town of Tuskegee. Tuskegee had some important advantages. It was located in the far southern United States, which meant its climate was warm. This allowed for year-round flying. Also, the Tuskegee Institute—complete with its CPTP—was already there. Building the field there would bring a large number of skilled African Americans to the area, and the local African-American community welcomed these newcomers with open arms.

A VISIT FROM THE FIRST LADY

Charles "Chief" Anderson joined the faculty at Tuskegee Institute as head of the CPTP in 1940. First Lady Eleanor Roosevelt visited Tuskegee in March 1941, determined to publicly oppose the notion that African Americans could not be aviators. She asked Anderson, "Can Negroes really fly airplanes?"[9] In reply, Anderson offered her a plane ride. She accepted, and up they went. After they landed, she said, "I guess Negroes can fly."[10] Then the two posed for pictures. Newspapers across the United States published their photograph and story, giving a big boost to African-American aviation.

But Tuskegee had one major drawback. The local white community was unwelcoming. Tuskegee was in the Deep South, where Jim Crow was still a reality. An influx of educated, confident African-American men threatened white supremacy there. Tuskegee cadets would come mostly from areas outside the

Not all students at Tuskegee piloted planes. Some studied aircraft maintenance.

Deep South. Though they had experience with racial discrimination and were familiar with Jim Crow, many were not familiar with the extent of violence and fear they would encounter in Alabama. Missteps could antagonize the local whites and prove dangerous or even deadly to the cadets.

Nonetheless, the plan went forward. By November 1941, TAAF was functional, and cadets began training there. The student body included not only pilot trainees, but also ground support personnel such as armorers, mechanics, meteorologists, parachute riggers, supply clerks, and welders. The first class of pilots graduated from TAAF training in March 1942.

Meanwhile, the United States had become directly involved in World War II. In December 1941, Japan had attacked Pearl Harbor, a major US military installation in Hawaii. In response, the United States declared war on Japan and sped up its military expansion. This expansion included three more African-American flight units, the 100th, 301st, and 302nd Fighter Squadrons, all established in 1942. The US Army Air Forces (USAAF, formerly the Army Air Corps) held tightly to its policy of segregation, so TAAF became crowded with cadets and airplanes. Graduations and commissioning ceremonies were happening every five or six weeks. TAAF was churning out qualified aviators, but the War Department was delaying sending these men into combat. This inefficiency brought intense public scrutiny during the first few months of 1943. Finally, in April 1943, the War Department sent the 100th, 301st, and 302nd—bound together as the 332nd Fighter Group—to Selfridge Field near Detroit, Michigan, to prepare for deployment overseas. And the Ninety-Ninth Fighter Squadron at last deployed to North Africa.

Their training complete, graduates of the Tuskegee program prepared for their first experiences in combat.

FROM AFRICA TO EUROPE

On April 2, 1943, the 400 men of the Ninety-Ninth Fighter Squadron left Tuskegee under the leadership of Lieutenant Colonel Benjamin O. Davis Jr. After a brief stay in New York, on April 15 the men boarded a troop transport with approximately 3,500 other men.[1] They crossed the Atlantic Ocean and arrived in Casablanca, Morocco, on April 24.

THE NORTH AFRICAN CAMPAIGN

In the early 1900s, all the countries of North Africa had come under the control of various European nations. By 1933, French Morocco was a colony of France. Spanish Morocco, the northernmost slice of the region, belonged to Spain. Algeria and

BENJAMIN O. DAVIS JR.

1912–2002

Benjamin O. Davis Jr. was born in Washington, DC, on December 18, 1912. Davis became interested in aviation at age 14, when a stunt pilot took him for a ride. In 1932, he entered the US Military Academy at West Point. He was the only African-American cadet there. For his entire four years at West Point, no one would room with him or speak to him outside the line of duty. "It was designed to make me buckle, but I refused to buckle," he said. "They didn't understand that I was going to stay there, and I was going to graduate."[2]

He graduated with a rank of 35 in a class of 276. Davis applied for a commission in the Army Air Corps but was rejected because he was an African American. Instead he was assigned to an all-African-American infantry unit as a second lieutenant. Davis was later transferred to Tuskegee for pilot training. He excelled in this training and was quickly promoted to lieutenant colonel and commander of the Ninety-Ninth Fighter Squadron.

After the war, Davis helped draft the US Air Force integration policy. In 1954, he became the first black general in the US Air Force. In 1967 he took command of the Thirteenth Air Force. He retired from the military in 1970. In 1998, President Bill Clinton advanced him to the rank of four-star general. Davis died on July 4, 2002, at the age of 89.

Tunisia were under French rule. Libya was an Italian colony, and Egypt belonged to the huge British Empire.

Soon after World War II broke out in 1939, the colonial powers began struggling for control of North Africa. Various locations in North Africa were important to European leaders because controlling these places affected travel on the Mediterranean Sea, passage through Egypt's Suez Canal to destinations in southern and eastern Asia, and access to oil supplies in the Middle East. From 1940 to 1943, Allied and Axis forces pushed one another back and forth across North Africa.

By the time the Ninety-Ninth Fighter Squadron arrived on the continent, the Allied North African campaign was winding down. This campaign was the Allies' effort to push Axis forces out of North Africa. The Allies had gained control of Morocco and Algeria in the west, as well as Libya and Egypt in the east. While the Allies fought for control of Tunisia, the Ninety-Ninth trained in Morocco in the airplanes they had just received for combat duty. These P-40 Warhawks were new airplanes, and the men of the Ninety-Ninth were glad to have them.

THE P-40 WARHAWK

The P-40 Warhawk was a tough fighter plane. It had an armored cockpit and engine. It could keep flying even when damaged and could fly in almost any climate. It was an excellent dive bomber and could make high-speed turns when flying level. Pilots liked it for all these reasons. Mechanics liked it because its engine was easy to maintain. A US-made plane, the distance it could fly before refueling was greater than that of most European fighters. It had two nose-mounted machine guns and either two or six wing-mounted machine guns. It also carried a 3,500-pound (1,600 kg) load of bombs. It could fly up to an altitude of 15,000 feet (4,600 m).[3]

By May 13, 1943, the Allies had wrested Tunisia from the Germans and Italians. Meanwhile, the Ninety-Ninth finished training. On May 31, the men traveled east by train and truck to Tunisia's Cape Bon. Cape Bon is a peninsula that extends from the northeastern coast of Tunisia toward the Italian island of Sicily. Cape Bon and Sicily lie approximately 90 miles (145 km) apart across a narrow waterway called the Strait of Sicily. In the middle of this strait lies the Italian island of Pantelleria. During World War II, Pantelleria was home to more than 10,000 Axis troops, an airfield, and a complex system of gun defenses and radar stations.[4]

Whoever controlled Pantelleria controlled the Strait of Sicily. The Allies needed to get hold of Pantelleria and the strait. Only then could they begin their next big move: an invasion of Italy. The

In Africa, the Tuskegee Airmen flew the rugged P-40 Warhawk.

Allies intended to gain control of Pantelleria with concentrated bombing. They code-named this air offensive Operation Corkscrew. It had begun on May 18. As soon as the men of the Ninety-Ninth settled in at Cape Bon, they would join in. This would be the Tuskegee Airmen's first combat mission.

OPERATION CORKSCREW

The Ninety-Ninth spent the first week or so of June 1943 dive-bombing Pantelleria's defenses. By now the Allies had mostly cleared the skies of enemy planes, so the fliers did not face much danger from above. But even with that advantage, dive-bombing in a P-40 was no easy task. It meant barreling earthward in a steep dive to approximately 3,000 feet (900 m), aiming the plane directly at the target, then dropping a 500-pound (220 kg) bomb and pulling up sharply. The pilot did this while facing antiaircraft fire from below and extreme physical stress on both the plane and his body. A mechanical failure or a pilot error while dive bombing meant ramming into the ground at top speed—a quick, fiery death. The Ninety-Ninth averaged two dive-bombing missions per day.[5]

On June 9, 1943, the Ninety-Ninth began flying another sort of mission as well: escorting bombers. They would eventually become famous for their performance in this role, but on their first bomber escort mission, some of the men made a mistake. Because bomber airplanes were not agile enough to defend themselves from enemy planes, fighter escorts were supposed to stay with the bombers in a protective formation no matter what happened. On June 9, 13 P-40s from the Ninety-Ninth escorted a squadron of A-20 Havoc bombers over Pantelleria. During the mission, four German fighters attacked. Five members of the Ninety-Ninth left formation and chased the Germans. Luckily nothing bad happened, and all the bombers and fighters made it back to base. No one repeated the mistake when they performed a similar mission the next day—or ever again, for that matter. But the five fighters had broken an important rule, and this blot on their record would cause them trouble later on.

In the meantime, though, all was well. On June 11, British ships loaded with troops approached Pantelleria for an invasion. They expected a bloodbath, but what they got was surrender. The only injury, according to one report, was caused by a mule that bit a soldier. Area commander Colonel J. R. Watkins sent Davis a message of congratulations "for the splendid part you played in the Pantelleria show. You have . . . come out of your initial christening into battle stronger qualified than ever. Your people have borne up well . . . and there is every reason to believe that with more experience you will take your place . . . along with the best of them."[6] Operation Corkscrew was a success, and so was the Ninety-Ninth Fighter Squadron.

MOMYER'S COMPLAINT

Colonel William Momyer, the commander of the white air group to which the Ninety-Ninth was often attached, attempted to discredit the Tuskegee Airmen. He recommended to General George Marshall that the Ninety-Ninth be taken out of combat due to poor performance. Among other negative claims, Momyer criticized the pilots for a lack of aggression.

Momyer had never mentioned any of this to Davis. Davis was livid. He defended his men to a War Department committee studying the use of African-American soldiers. Marshall ordered a congressional hearing, which eventually rated the Ninety-Ninth Fighter Squadron's performance equal to those of other air units in the Mediterranean. The authorities removed the unit from Momyer's fighter group.

OPERATION HUSKY

After gaining control of Pantelleria, the Allies set their eyes on the much

Allied pilots painted Nazi symbols called swastikas on their planes for each German aircraft they shot down.

larger island of Sicily. This invasion, code-named Operation Husky, began with bombardment from the sea and the air.

On June 29, the Ninety-Ninth began flying bomber escort missions between Tunisia and Sicily. A few days later, on July 2, the Tuskegee Airmen experienced a pair of important firsts. One was triumphant, and the other was sobering. Twelve planes from the Ninety-Ninth departed Tunisia on a mission escorting

Pilots learned about the day's objectives at meetings before each mission.

12 B-25s to bomb an enemy airfield in southwestern Sicily. As the formation approached their target, German fighters attacked, then flew away. The Allied planes completed their bombing run and turned back toward base. Suddenly two

German planes reappeared. First Lieutenant Charles B. Hall of the Ninety-Ninth blasted one of them with his machine gun and witnessed its crash. This was the Tuskegee Airmen's first confirmed kill. Another pilot of the Ninety-Ninth, Lieutenant W. I. Lawson, shot at the other German plane. He saw smoke billow from it and watched it careen earthward. But because the crash happened out of sight, it was counted as a probable kill, not a confirmed one. In the confusion of the fight, two other planes from the Ninety-Ninth collided in midair. First Lieutenant Sherman H. White and Second Lieutenant James L. McCullin were the first Tuskegee Airmen killed in combat.

The ground invasion of Sicily began with airborne landings on July 9 and seaborne landings on July 10. The Ninety-Ninth provided air cover for these landings, keeping enemy aircraft away from the ships and beaches. Throughout July and into August, British and American forces made their way slowly across Sicily, and the Ninety-Ninth continued providing air cover. By the time the last Axis forces evacuated to the Italian mainland in mid-August, approximately 26,000 Allied and Axis soldiers were dead. For its excellent performance in the taking of Sicily, the Ninety-Ninth Fighter Squadron earned a Distinguished Unit Citation.

SUITING UP

For the pilots of the Ninety-Ninth Fighter Squadron, suiting up for a mission was no simple task. Even if ground conditions were blazing hot, conditions high in the air were usually freezing. The pilots wore bulky, lined lambskin pants and jackets. They strapped themselves into their seats and then donned their headgear. Because the air was thin at high altitude, pilots had to wear oxygen masks. They also wore goggles to protect their eyes and helmets to warm and protect their heads.

In late 1943, Allied troops and equipment began streaming ashore during the invasion of Italy.

THE ITALIAN CAMPAIGN

Not long after Axis forces evacuated from Sicily to mainland Italy, the Allies followed them. The Allies' plan was to gain control of the entire Italian Peninsula. They knew this would be a long and difficult effort, but it was important for several reasons. An invasion of Italy would give the Allies a foothold in Europe, forcing the Axis to act defensively instead of offensively. It would also expand Allied control in the Mediterranean, providing air bases within range of bombing targets behind enemy lines. Finally, opening a new fighting front in Europe would draw some Axis troops to Italy, relieving pressure on the Soviets fighting in Eastern Europe.

FROM MESSINA TO THE GUSTAV LINE

On September 2, 1943, the Army Air Forces called Davis back to the United States to take command of the 332nd Fighter Group. The

332nd, composed of the all-African-American 100th, 301st, and 302nd Fighter Squadrons, had completed training and was waiting to deploy at Selfridge Field in Michigan. It would be Davis's job to get the 332nd ready for deployment, accompany it to Italy, and lead it in combat. Meanwhile, African-American Major George S. "Spanky" Roberts took over command of the Ninety-Ninth Fighter Squadron, which had moved its base of operations from Tunisia to Sicily.

GEOGRAPHY OF ITALY

Italy was hard for the Allies to invade and easy for the Axis to defend because of its terrain. It has a central spine of mountains called the Apennines, which soar up to 10,000 feet (3,048 m). The Apennines have spurs that run east and west toward both coasts. Valleys between the mountains contain wide, fast-flowing rivers. The north-south roads hug the coastlines, and the bridges that carry these roads over the rivers are shielded by nearby mountains.

On September 3, Allied forces arrived at Reggio di Calabria, on the toe of boot-shaped Italy. On September 8, the Italian government surrendered. Germany immediately sent troops to occupy the country and defend against the Allied invasion. The next day, separate Allied forces landed at Taranto, on the heel of Italy, and Salerno, on the ankle. Their goal was to capture Naples, a vital port on Italy's western coast approximately 35 miles (56 km) north of Salerno. The Allies faced no opposition except at Salerno. German forces had been expecting this landing, and they defended the beach fiercely. But thanks to the Allies' naval gunfire and air support, they were able to overcome the Germans by September 15. The Germans withdrew to the Gustav Line, a mountainous defensive line crossing the Italian Peninsula, which was anchored by the fortress

Italian Campaign Map

Ground crews were critical to the success of the Tuskegee Airmen.

of Monte Cassino. Meanwhile, the Allies advanced northward. By October 1, they had captured Naples in the west and the airfields at Foggia in the east.

During the Allied advance to Naples and Foggia, the Tuskegee Airmen of the Ninety-Ninth continued escorting bombers on raids over mainland Italy. They also performed patrol missions, keeping the skies clear of enemy planes while Allied troops marched northward on the ground. On October 16, the Ninety-Ninth was reassigned to a group commanded by Colonel Earl Bates. The next day, the Ninety-Ninth pulled up roots and moved to a new base of operations at Foggia. Once settled, the men continued providing close air support for Allied troops on the ground. They also attacked strategic targets, such as ammunition storage sites and enemy shipping operations.

For the rest of 1943, the Allied and Axis forces stood more or less at a stalemate. The Allies kept attacking the Gustav Line in an attempt to capture their next big objective: Rome, the capital city of Italy. Meanwhile, the Axis troops dug in their heels and tried to outlast the attacks. The Ninety-Ninth moved two more times, eventually landing on January 16, 1944, at the Capodichino Airdrome near Naples.

WHO WERE THE TUSKEGEE AIRMEN?

Although the name Tuskegee Airmen brings to mind the African-American pilots of World War II, it refers to many other soldiers as well. All the ground personnel necessary for self-contained African-American air units were also Tuskegee Airmen. These included administrative clerks, air traffic controllers, armament specialists, bombardiers, communications specialists, cooks, electricians, firefighters, flight instructors, laboratory assistants, mechanics, medics, musicians, navigators, parachute riggers, policemen, radio repairmen and technicians, supply and transportation personnel, and many other positions.

From there, the Ninety-Ninth would participate in a new effort to reach Rome, which lay 140 miles (225 km) northwest along the coast.[1]

FROM THE GUSTAV LINE TO ROME

On January 22, the Allies launched an attack by sea on Anzio, 30 miles (48 km) south of Rome. They successfully landed 70,000 soldiers, but those soldiers ended up stranded on the beachhead, surrounded by German forces.[2] The Allied troops were pushed back, but they later regrouped. It took four more months for Allied ground troops to break through the Gustav Line. When this finally happened in May, causing the Germans to retreat farther north, the Allied forces at Anzio pushed forward. They eventually linked up with their comrades headed north from the Gustav Line, and together these troops marched into Rome on June 4.

In the skies over Anzio, the Tuskegee Airmen at last got a chance to show what they could do. On January 27 and 28, 16 members of the Ninety-Ninth were flying a patrol mission over an Allied fleet south of Anzio. They spotted 15 German aircraft dive-bombing Allied ships near the beaches of Anzio. The Americans chased the Germans. During the ensuing dogfight, ten Tuskegee Airmen shot down ten enemy airplanes. The Ninety-Ninth did not escape unscathed, though. Lieutenant Samuel F. Bruce bailed out of his destroyed plane, but his parachute failed, and he was killed.

The next day, the Ninety-Ninth flew another mission over Anzio. Several enemy fighters appeared, and another dogfight followed. The Americans shot down three of the Germans. Two of those kills went to Charles B. Hall, the pilot who had made the Ninety-Ninth's first kill back on July 2, 1943. This raised

US pilots, seeing bombs explode around Allied ships near Anzio, engaged the German attack aircraft in the area.

Hall's total to three and earned him the Distinguished Flying Cross. In two days, the Tuskegee Airmen had shot down 13 enemy airplanes.[3] The accomplishment went a long way toward quieting their critics.

PRISONERS OF WAR

On August 12, 1944, the 332nd attacked German radar stations in southern France, near Marseilles. Lieutenants Alexander Jefferson, Robert Daniels Jr., and Richard Macon were shot down and became prisoners of war in Germany. Although the Nazis' hatred for blacks was well-known, Jefferson said:

The only time I really became frightened was . . . when . . . we were accosted by a group of Hitler Youth. . . . When they spotted us they began yelling obscenities. . . . They called us Luftgangster (air gangsters) and Terrorflieger (pilots of terror) and all kinds of other things. . . . You're damn right I was scared. We had heard of downed Allied flying personnel being beaten and even murdered by angry German civilians. After all, what would American citizens have done to German airmen who had just bombed their homes and cities?[4]

ROME, BERLIN, HOME

While the Ninety-Ninth Fighter Squadron was busy shooting down German fighters, patrolling, and dive-bombing in early 1944, the 332nd Fighter Group was approaching Italy. From February 1 to February 3, the group's three squadrons arrived in various places on the Italian mainland. They then traveled to their base at Montecorvino, where they all arrived by February 8. All the Tuskegee Airmen knew the rallying cry of the Allied soldiers in Europe at this time: "Rome, Berlin, home!" This meant they knew their job was to defeat both Italy and Germany. Only then would they go home to their loved ones.

For the 332nd's first month, they spent time getting used to their airplanes, P-39 Airacobras, and flying in the crowded skies of the combat zone. By March they were ready to venture out of the rear area

The Airacobra saw service all over the world, from Italy to Alaska to the Soviet Union.

Bright red tails became the easily recognizable signature of the Tuskegee Airmen.

and into full combat duty. Similar to their fellow fliers in the Ninety-Ninth, they escorted bombers, went on dive-bombing missions, and patrolled the skies, providing air cover for ground operations.

Not long after the Allies took Rome in early June, the Ninety-Ninth was added to the 332nd Fighter Group, commanded by Davis. In July 1944, they took up lodgings together at Ramitelli Airfield on the eastern coast of Italy. The men generally saw this combining of African-American squadrons as a step backward. It meant the War Department was determined to keep them segregated from the rest of the US Army pilots. But the development had its advantages. It placed all the Tuskegee men under Davis, a highly skilled leader they all respected. And it brought them new airplanes, too. Now they would be flying P-51 Mustangs, widely considered the best fighter planes of the war.

The men of the 332nd decided to give their new planes distinctive markings so they would be able to identify one another in combat. It also meant friendly bomber crews and enemy fighters would remember them. They had no particular design in mind at first. When they visited the nearest supply depot, they found

THE AIRMEN ON FILM

The Tuskegee Airmen and their famous red-tailed planes have appeared onscreen numerous times over the decades, in movies ranging from documentaries to big-budget Hollywood productions. One of their first appearances on film came in the 1945 short documentary *Wings for This Man*, produced by the US government to showcase the achievements of the pilots to the US public. Narrated by actor and eventual US president Ronald Reagan, the movie features footage from training and combat. While not mentioning racism directly, the narration notes "You can't judge a man here by the color of his eyes or the shape of his nose. On the flight strip, you judge a man by the way he flies."[5]

Maintenance crews kept the Tuskegee Airmen's planes running smoothly in harsh wartime conditions.

a huge store of bright red paint. They brushed it onto all their planes' tails, wingtips, and nose spinners. It was not long before they were known throughout the European theater of war as Red Tails.

From this point onward, the role of the 332nd changed. The airmen now flew mostly bomber escort missions behind enemy lines. In this role, their outstanding performance made them famous. Their easily recognizable planes filled the German pilots with fear and gave the Allied bomber crews confidence. One pilot of a B-24 bomber explained the difference between the Red Tails and the other bomber escorts—and it had nothing to do with the color of their planes or their skin:

> The P-38s always stayed too far out. Some of the Mustang group stayed in too close. . . . Other groups, we got the feeling that they just wanted to go and shoot down 109s. . . . The Red Tails were always out there where we wanted them to be. . . . We had no idea they were Black; it was the Army's best kept secret.[6]

As summer turned to fall and then winter, the Red Tails and other Allied aircraft carried on a relentless assault against the remaining Axis forces in northern Italy and beyond. The damage they wrought on enemy infrastructure eventually brought the German forces in Italy to their knees, and they surrendered on May 2, 1945. Six days later, the entire German military surrendered to the Allies, and the war in Europe was over.

The Tuskegee Airmen had gone into combat facing major challenges. They knew their work was deadly, and many of their fellow soldiers did not accept them. They also knew that if they performed well in combat, they would show

When flying bomber escort missions in Germany, P-51s were often equipped with extra fuel tanks on their wings to increase their flight range.

the decision to train and deploy them had been the right one. This might open up more opportunities for African Americans both in the military and in civilian society. In other words, they had a lot to prove. They proved it well, with an outstanding total record of 112 enemy aircraft shot down.[7]

TUSKEGEE AIRMEN COMBAT RECORD

15,000-plus combat sorties

950 motor vehicles destroyed

744 Air Medals earned

150 Distinguished Flying Crosses earned

150 enemy airplanes destroyed on the ground

112 enemy airplanes destroyed in the air

352 pilots deployed for combat in Europe

66 pilots killed in combat

32 pilots downed and captured

14 Bronze Stars earned

8 Purple Hearts earned

1 destroyer sunk[8]

New classes of Tuskegee Airmen continued to train throughout the war.

THE HOME FRONT

While the Red Tails dazzled everyone in the skies over Europe, more Tuskegee Airmen continued training back at home in the United States. In some respects, the home front was a more difficult environment for African-American soldiers than the combat zone. By and large, white Americans still viewed African Americans as inferior. Racial discrimination and segregation were still entrenched in US law and society. These realities affected the experiences of airmen posted at Tuskegee Army Air Field and other military facilities in the United States.

BURSTING AT THE SEAMS

By late 1943, the USAAF had organized the Ninety-Ninth Fighter Squadron and the three squadrons of the 332nd Fighter Group and had deployed all four of these squadrons into combat. In addition, it was training replacement personnel for these squadrons. And because the USAAF had a policy of segregating black units, all African-American replacement pilots were training at Tuskegee. By 1944, TAAF was overflowing with new recruits.

Overcrowding at Tuskegee was unpleasant. It was also humiliating, because it showed the men stationed there the government would rather crowd them into a single facility than let them work alongside white aviators. The unpleasantness and humiliation lowered morale.

INVENTING JOBS

TAAF was so overcrowded that for every officer's job that needed to be done, five or six officers were available. To cope with the ridiculous situation, TAAF invented positions such as Assistant Post Beautification Officer, Assistant to the Assistant Mess Officer, and Assistant to the Assistant Supply Officer.

Overcrowding was also inefficient—and therefore costly. The USAAF had several airfields for training white pilots, but it insisted African-American pilots could train only at Tuskegee. At its peak, TAAF had 600 cadets in various stages of training, ranging from those taking their first college classes to fully trained graduates.[1] The classrooms and runways suffered from constant traffic jams. This slowed down the training process, which in turn made the crowding worse.

Because the training process was so slow, TAAF could not produce new pilots as quickly as they were needed. Flying fighters was exhausting, dangerous work. After flying approximately 50 missions, pilots normally got a rest by rotating back home for a new assignment—oftentimes training upcoming pilots. But in World War II, African-American pilots typically had to fly 70 or 80 combat missions before rotating stateside.[2] Their exhaustion added an unnecessary layer of challenge to an already difficult job.

THE 477TH BOMBARDMENT GROUP

In late 1943, the USAAF came under increasing pressure to create more black combat units. There were so many airmen at Tuskegee, and the need for new pilots was so great, that even the most prejudiced officials could not make a good argument for limiting the number of African-American airmen in combat. The result was the creation of the 477th Bombardment Group.

Once the 332nd Fighter Group left Selfridge Field for deployment in December 1943, the USAAF activated the 477th Bombardment Group at Selfridge in January 1944. Racial tensions were high in the Detroit area at that time. The 477th's white commander, Colonel

The Tuskegee Airmen would face severe racism at Michigan's Selfridge Field.

Robert Selway Jr., made things even more tense for the airmen with a speech he made upon their arrival. He reminded them they were not equal to whites, he would not tolerate race-mixing, and African-American officers could not use the officers' club. He warned anyone protesting these conditions would be disciplined. Colonel William Boyd, the commanding officer of Selfridge Field, supported Selway's stance.

Selway and Boyd had created an impossible, illogical situation. Officers' clubs were not just places to hang out and relax. Traditionally, when a commanding officer went to the club, all the officers under him went along, and they stayed as long as he stayed. In this way, the officers' club played a key role in unit bonding. By telling black officers they could not use the Selfridge officers' club, Selway and Boyd not only damaged relationships within the 477th but also implied its officers were not really officers.

RACIAL UNREST IN DETROIT

In June 1943, a riot broke out between whites and African Americans in Detroit. It got too big for the police and state troops to control. US Army soldiers had to intervene and restore order.

Around the same time at Selfridge Field, a white officer shot and wounded an African-American enlisted man. The officer was punished, but his sentence was outrageously minor. He simply had his rank reduced from colonel to captain.

GODMAN FIELD

In May 1944, the 477th moved to Godman Field in Kentucky, partly for the warmer climate and partly to get away from the racial unrest in Detroit. Selway found a workaround to keep the black and white officers from socializing together. The African Americans were welcome at the officers' club on base, but only the white officers were ever invited as guests to the officers' club at adjacent Fort Knox. Thus the white officers always used the Fort Knox officers' club, while the black officers used the club at Godman Field.

Meanwhile, the group's preparation for combat limped slowly along. Bombardment group training was slower than that of fighter groups. Bomber aircraft required pilots, navigators, bombardiers, radio operators, and gunners— all of whom needed individual training and then cooperative training. And due to the training backlog at Tuskegee, the 477th could not get enough of all the right kinds of airmen to complete the group.

FREEMAN FIELD

In March 1945, the 477th finally reached full combat strength and moved again—this time to Freeman Field in Indiana. Freeman was a larger base, so Selway designated two different buildings as officers' clubs. He said one would be for training officers and the other for trainees. But segregation was clearly the real reason for having two clubs. This violated the current USAAF regulation, which prohibited the use of the facility's buildings for any social purpose "unless all officers on duty at the post [were granted] the right to full membership."[3] Sick of this blatant, repeated, and insulting violation of their rights, in early April many of the African-American officers requested entry at the club and were refused. They entered anyway, and dozens were arrested. Later, when ordered to sign a statement saying they had read and understood an order of restriction written by Selway, many of the black officers refused. This showed how serious they were about ending segregation. Refusal to obey a direct order from a

Keep us flying!

BUY WAR BONDS

superior during wartime is a serious military offense.

The USAAF reprimanded the dissenters, but it did not want to cause an uproar by handing down harsh punishments. Instead, to resolve the racial conflict, the arrested officers were transferred back to Godman Field in late April. Selway and all the other white officers were replaced by Colonel Davis, who had returned from Europe, and other black officers.

On May 7, Nazi Germany surrendered to the Allies. With the war in Europe over, the 477th would now prepare for combat against Japan. Davis returned from Europe in August 1945, and the 477th was set to deploy by late August. Japan informally surrendered on August 14, 1945, and formally surrendered on September 2, 1945,

US government posters highlighted the achievements of the Tuskegee Airmen, but the pilots still faced discrimination.

CONTRASTING COMMANDERS

Tuskegee saw its share of racial tension, too. After all, TAAF was crowded with approximately 2,000 African-American soldiers and surrounded by a hostile white community.[4] But Colonel Noel Parrish handled racial tensions quite differently than Selway did.

On August 3, 1944, 12 African American officers walked into the "whites only" section of a restaurant on the TAAF grounds. They asked to be served. A white officer asked them to go to the "blacks only" section of the restaurant. The African-American officers showed him two letters from the War Department stating service at base recreational facilities could not be refused due to race. Colonel Parrish encouraged the white officer to let the black officers be served wherever they liked. As a result, the restaurant became peacefully racially integrated.

ending World War II. After all it had endured at home in the United States, the 477th never got a chance to fight in Europe.

The pilots were glad to arrive home, but they soon found racist attitudes had changed little during the war.

CHAPTER
★ 8 ★

POSTWAR CHALLENGES

After World War II ended, the Red Tails returned home to the United States. Meanwhile, thousands of Tuskegee Airmen were still training or were awaiting deployment. Counting all the pilots and support personnel in all stages of training and service, the Tuskegee Airmen added up to approximately 19,000 soldiers.[1] They all wondered what would become of them.

One thing was certain: racial discrimination was still present in US society. Despite their outstanding combat record and their high levels of education and skill, the Tuskegee Airmen continued to face discrimination in both society and the military, especially during the first few years after the war. It was a bitter pill to swallow after all their hard work and sacrifice.

CIVILIAN PURSUITS

The US armed forces shrank drastically after the war, so many of the Tuskegee Airmen returned to civilian life simply because the military no longer needed them. In addition, many Tuskegee Airmen had never meant to spend their lives in the military. Some had been drafted. Others had joined the military out of a sense of duty and patriotism. Still others had enlisted specifically to take advantage of the education and training offered through the Tuskegee program. Whatever their reasons for serving, they were ready to leave, and they hoped their service would open at least a few minds and new opportunities.

For many African-American soldiers, hopes about open minds were dashed quickly. Joseph Shambrey, a mechanic who had been stationed in Italy with the Red Tails, was one of them. He returned to Alabama after his tour of duty. He got off a train at his destination and spotted a hospitality station. Volunteers at the station welcomed returning white soldiers with handshakes and free coffee.

FRIENDS UNTIL THE END

Joseph Shambrey and Clarence E. Huntley Jr. grew up in the same neighborhood of Los Angeles, California. In high school during the 1930s, they ran track together. And when World War II erupted, they enlisted together. They were both eager to participate in the Tuskegee program and get trained as aircraft mechanics—and both got accepted. They deployed to Italy together. Both survived, and they returned home together to marry the sweethearts they had left behind. When the United States entered the Korean War, Shambrey and Huntley both shipped out overseas as combat engineers. Once again, they both survived. They returned home, took civilian jobs, and stayed friends, never letting a month pass without a visit or a phone call. In fact, their friendship lasted right until the very end—they both died on January 5, 2015.

Some Tuskegee Airmen, including General Daniel James Jr., *right*, remained in the military for decades following their World War II service.

But when Shambrey and his fellow Tuskegee Airmen disembarked, they got no congratulations—and they had to pay for their coffee.

Similarly, hopes for new and better employment opportunities were quickly dashed. As military personnel were discharged postwar, the race barrier grew taller. Racial discrimination became a huge hurdle to African Americans looking for jobs in the private sector.

Lieutenant Colonel Asa "Ace" Herring, a Tuskegee pilot, recalled the prospects for pilots were especially disappointing. "The training was more than the usual for a pilot," he explained. However, he said, "We didn't have the [job] opportunities that some of the others had."[2] Black pilots were prohibited from flying commercial aircraft—a ban that continued until 1963. A key path to professional and financial success was closed to Tuskegee pilots. "Airline pilots make good money. Certainly back in those days it was considered a glamour job," said Ken Rapier, cousin of Tuskegee pilot Gordon Rapier.[3] "We felt dejected," said Herring, "and certainly we didn't enjoy the discriminatory practices that were prevalent during that era."[4]

MILITARY CAREERS

Some Tuskegee Airmen stayed in the military because jobs, pay, and treatment were slightly better in the military than in civilian society. But for the first few years after the war, the military remained segregated. Opportunities for advancement were limited. In fact, some Tuskegee Airmen were forced to take assignments well beneath their qualifications.

Herring's fellow pilot Lieutenant Colonel Robert Ashby was one of these. Ashby, similar to many Tuskegee Airmen, decided to stick it out in the USAAF.

Herring, *second from left*, reunited with other surviving Tuskegee Airmen in 2012.

More than 60 years later, Ashby related his experiences with the Tuskegee Airmen in a speech at the Arizona State Capitol.

It deployed him for the postwar occupation of Japan. But despite his proven skill at flying several different types of aircraft, he was given a ground assignment rather than a job flying. In a word, he said, this assignment made him feel "lousy."[5]

Tuskegee Airmen who continued to fly served in all-African-American units. The USAAF closed Tuskegee Army Air Field in March 1946. At that point, the USAAF moved all its segregated flying units—both fighter and bomber squadrons—to Lockbourne Army Air Field near Columbus, Ohio. Ashby joined them there in 1948, and Lockbourne remained segregated until July 1949. But change was coming for African Americans in the military.

A FIRST FOR ROBERT ASHBY

Ashby went on to serve for 21 years in the military. After he retired, he flew in the commercial airline industry. First, he took a job as a flight operation instructor with United Airlines. Later, he became a pilot with Frontier Airlines. He was the first and only Tuskegee Airman known to have made a career as a commercial airline pilot.

Through their impressive service record, the Tuskegee Airmen helped disprove racist notions about African Americans in the military.

LEGACY OF THE TUSKEGEE AIRMEN

In the face of many obstacles, the Tuskegee Airmen performed extremely well. They proved to the American public they were effective aviators—equal to white pilots and support troops. Given the opportunity, they showed intelligence, skill, bravery, leadership, and integrity. The Tuskegee Airmen's stellar performance made their segregated status look illogical, if not downright immoral. Fortunately, some government and military leaders were paying attention.

PRESSURE FOR CHANGE

Pressure for change came from multiple groups of people with a variety of motives. African-American veterans themselves made up one of these groups. They pled for an end to discrimination in the armed forces.

Civilian organizations spoke up as well. The National Association for the Advancement of Colored People, the National Urban League, and individual civil rights leaders such as A. Philip Randolph pressed for action. They urged President Harry S. Truman to extend the protections from racial discrimination enjoyed by African-American employees in private companies building war weapons and vehicles—protections put into place by Roosevelt—to members of the military.

Some key military leaders made a compelling case for integration, too. Their influence was, perhaps, the most critical. While many military leaders may have felt, as Secretary of the Army Kenneth Royall did, that the military "was not an instrument for social evolution," others argued segregation was inefficient, costly, and counterproductive.[1] Colonel Noel Parrish was a vocal member of this group. He hated the "terribly expensive [and] disturbing aspects of trying to operate

EMBARRASSING QUESTIONS

In 1945 Abol Amini, a member of the Iranian parliament, visited Tuskegee Army Air Field with a group of Iranians led by the US State Department. Amini kept asking embarrassing questions: "Why were [African-American] pilots and officers kept apart [from] the rest of the Air Forces? Were they not also citizens of a democracy? Could the reason be that their complexions were dark?"[2] Telling this story later, Parrish revealed that many foreign visitors to TAAF asked similar questions. He lamented, "Most Americans in authority seem to forget that foreign visitors have read our Constitution."[3]

Parrish, *right*, was one of the few commanders who believed African-American pilots could perform as well as their white counterparts.

an Air Force within an Air Force with a separate personnel system, a separate training system, a separate everything."[4] He pointed out the US Air Force was spending at least three or four times as much per African-American pilot as it was spending per white pilot.[5]

INTEGRATION AT LAST

Government and military leaders found Parrish's arguments persuasive. On December 5, 1946, President Truman established the President's Committee on Civil Rights. The committee's job was to suggest ways to strengthen and protect the civil rights of all Americans. The committee's investigations and discussions led to a report issued in October 1947. The report recommended ending "immediately all discrimination and segregation based on race, color, creed or national origin in . . . all branches of the Armed Services."[6]

US senators from the South resisted this proposal. But acting as the commander in chief of the nation's armed forces, Truman went around the pro-segregation senators by issuing an executive order on July 26, 1948. Executive Order 9981 stated, "It is herby declared to be the policy of the President that there shall be equality of treatment and opportunity for all persons in the Armed Services without regard to race."[7] It took the various military branches several years to implement Truman's order. The US Air Force was the first branch to integrate in 1949. The Korean War (1950–1953) brought a new need for combat troops, pushing the other branches to integrate. In 1954, the US Army was the last branch of the US military to become desegregated.

During the Korean War, white and African-American pilots finally got to serve alongside each other.

The Tuskegee Airmen have been honored with medals and other awards in the decades following their service.

Airman Herring remembered thinking Truman's order was a step forward, but also that it was "just a piece of paper. It doesn't change the hearts and minds of the people, and therefore, it was a gradual change."[8]

However, airman Ashby pointed out, "I would say the greatest contribution we made to this country is we integrated the military."[9] Many Americans agree. Without the Tuskegee Airmen, who helped establish diversity and tolerance in the military, the civil rights era might have happened differently. Modern leaders still recognize the important role these soldiers played more than 70 years ago. President Barack Obama, the first African-American president of the United States, wrote that his "career in public service was made possible by the path heroes like the Tuskegee Airmen trail-blazed."[10]

CONGRESSIONAL GOLD MEDAL

In March 2007, decades after the Tuskegee Airmen's missions over Italy and Germany, the men were recognized for their service to the country. The US Congress collectively awarded them the Congressional Gold Medal, one of the highest civilian honors in the United States. In giving the award to the airmen, Congress recognized "their unique military record, which inspired revolutionary reform in the Armed Forces."[11] The medal was put on display at the Smithsonian Institution in Washington, DC.

TIMELINE

1775–1783
Approximately 5,000 African Americans serve in the Revolutionary War.

1861–1865
The US Civil War takes place. Many African-American soldiers and sailors fight for the Union.

1865–1877
Reconstruction occurs in the South; briefly, conditions improve dramatically for African Americans.

1896
The US Supreme Court rules "separate but equal" facilities are constitutional.

1941
The US War Department announces the creation of an all-African-American fighter squadron.

1942
The first class of pilots graduates from the Tuskegee Army Air Field.

1943
The Ninety-Ninth Fighter Squadron deploys to North Africa.

1944
The 332nd Fighter Group deploys to Italy and unites with the Ninety-Ninth Fighter Squadron at Ramitelli Airfield.

1917–1918

Four hundred thousand African Americans serve in the US military during US participation in World War I.

1925

The US Army War College publishes a study concerning African-American soldiers.

1939

World War II begins; the Civilian Pilot Training Program at the Tuskegee Institute begins in December.

1940

The United States begins drafting men. Official policy excludes African Americans from the Army Air Corps.

1945

African-American officers are arrested at Freeman Field in Indiana; Germany and Japan both surrender.

1946

Tuskegee Army Air Field closes; President Harry S. Truman establishes the President's Committee on Civil Rights.

1948

President Truman eliminates segregation in the US military with Executive Order 9981.

1949

The US Air Force becomes the first branch of the military to desegregate.

ESSENTIAL FACTS

KEY PLAYERS

- Charles "Chief" Anderson heads the Civilian Pilot Training Program at the Tuskegee Institute.

- Benjamin O. Davis Jr. leads the Ninety-Ninth Fighter Squadron and the 332nd Fighter Group.

- William Momyer commands the air group to which the Tuskegee Airmen were attached and attempted to discredit the African-American pilots.

- Harry S. Truman desegregates the US armed forces by executive order in 1948.

KEY STATISTICS

- The P-51 Mustang could fly at nearly 440 miles per hour (708 kmh).

- The Tuskegee Airmen flew more than 15,000 combat sorties.

- The Tuskegee Airmen shot down a total of 112 enemy aircraft.

IMPACT ON THE WAR

As Allied ground forces fought their way across Sicily and Italy, the Tuskegee Airmen provided crucial support from the air. They later escorted bombers on dangerous flights over Germany, protecting the vulnerable aircraft from German fighters. Their work saved the lives of many fellow Allied soldiers, both in the air and on the ground.

LEGACY OF THE TUSKEGEE AIRMEN

The stellar performance of the Tuskegee Airmen in World War II helped disprove racist notions about the inferiority of African-American pilots. Their successes led directly to the integration of the US military and indirectly to the US civil rights movement. On May 27, 2009, the US Congress awarded the Tuskegee Airmen a Congressional Gold Medal, one of the highest civilian honors available.

QUOTE

"It was designed to make me buckle, but I refused to buckle. They didn't understand that I was going to stay there, and I was going to graduate."

—*Benjamin O. Davis on the discrimination he faced at West Point*

GLOSSARY

BOMBARDIER
A bomber aircraft crew member who controls the aircraft and releases bombs while over the target area.

BOMBER
An airplane, such as the B-24 or B-25, designed for dropping bombs. Bombers in World War II typically carried crews of six to ten men.

CADET
A student or trainee in the armed services.

DISCRIMINATION
Treating some people better than others without any fair or proper reason.

DOGFIGHT
An aerial battle between single opposing planes or groups of planes.

ENLIST
To enter a nation's military.

FORMATION
An arrangement of airplanes.

GROUP
A unit in the US Army Air Forces consisting of three squadrons.

INFRASTRUCTURE

The physical structures, such as roads, railways, and power plants, that make it possible for a city or nation to function.

INTEGRATION

Acceptance of people belonging to different groups (such as races) as equals in society.

NAVIGATOR

A crew member on a bomber airplane who is responsible for determining the location and direction of the aircraft and the target.

SEGREGATION

The separation or isolation of a race, class, or group.

SORTIE

A mission by a single unit, such as a plane, against enemy forces. For military fliers, a sortie is a flight intended to meet enemy aircraft or to carry out bombing of an enemy target.

SQUADRON

A unit in the US Army Air Forces consisting of 12 to 24 aircraft.

ADDITIONAL RESOURCES

SELECTED BIBLIOGRAPHY

Moye, J. Todd. *Freedom Flyers: The Tuskegee Airmen of World War II*. New York: Oxford UP, 2010. Print.

Sandler, Stanley. *Segregated Skies: All-Black Combat Squadrons of WWII*. Washington, DC: Smithsonian, 1992. Print.

Stentiford, Barry M. *Tuskegee Airmen*. Santa Barbara, CA: ABC-CLIO, 2012. Print.

FURTHER READINGS

Brown, Nikki L. M., and Barry M. Stentiford, Editors. *Jim Crow: A Historical Encyclopedia of the American Mosaic*. Santa Barbara, CA: ABC-CLIO, 2014. Print.

Caver, Joseph, Jerome Ennels, and Daniel Haulman. *The Tuskegee Airmen: An Illustrated History*. Montgomery, AL: NewSouth, 2011. Print.

Earl, Sari. *Benjamin O. Davis Jr.: Air Force General and Tuskegee Airmen Leader*. Minneapolis: Abdo, 2010. Print.

WEBSITES

To learn more about Essential Library of World War II, visit **booklinks.abdopublishing.com**. These links are routinely monitored and updated to provide the most current information available.

PLACES TO VISIT

Smithsonian National Air and Space Museum
Independence Avenue at Sixth Street Southwest
Washington, DC 20560
202-633-2214
http://airandspace.si.edu
Among the most popular museums in the world, the Air and Space Museum includes aircraft from World War II, including P-51s like the ones flown by the Tuskegee Airmen.

Tuskegee Airmen National Historic Site
1616 Chappie James Avenue
Tuskegee, Alabama 36083
334-724-0922
http://www.nps.gov/tuai/index.htm
The area where Tuskegee Airmen trained for flight is now open to the public as a memorial for the pioneering African-American pilots.

SOURCE NOTES

CHAPTER 1. RED-TAIL ANGELS

1. Gabrielle Fimbres. "A Tuskegee Airman Appeared—and WWII Bomb Crew Was Saved." *Arizona Daily Star*. Arizona Daily Star, 10 Feb. 2013. Web. 19 Dec. 2014.

2. Ibid.

3. "North American P-51D Mustang." *National Museum of the US Air Force*. National Museum of the US Air Force, 14 July 2014. Web. 13 Apr. 2015.

4. Noble Frankland. "Comments: Lieutenant General Ira C. Eaker." *US Air Force*. US Air Force, 1968. Web. 22 Dec. 2014.

CHAPTER 2. THE LONG ROAD TO TAKEOFF

1. "Declaration of Independence." *National Archives: The Charters of Freedom*. National Archives, n.d. Web. 15 Jan. 2015.

2. "George Fitzhugh, 'The Universal Law of Slavery (1850).'" *America: A Narrative History*. Norton, 2007. Web. 13 Apr. 2015.

3. "Rebuilding the Old Order." *US History*. Independence Hall Association, 2014. Web. 14 Apr. 2015.

4. "Jim Crow Era." *Jim Crow Museum*. Ferris State University, 2014. Web. 17 Jan. 2015.

CHAPTER 3. AFRICAN AMERICANS IN THE MILITARY

1. "Black Americans in Defense of Our Nation." *Sam Houston State University*. Department of Defense, 1985. Web. 18 Jan. 2015.

2. Ibid.

3. Ibid.

4. Ibid.

5. Craig Lloyd. "Eugene Bullard (1895–1961)." *New Georgia Encyclopedia*. New Georgia Encyclopedia, 2 Oct. 2014. Web. 19 Jan. 2015.

6. "Black Americans in Defense of Our Nation." *Sam Houston State University*. Department of Defense, 1985. Web. 18 Jan. 2015.

CHAPTER 4. FLIGHT TRAINING AT TUSKEGEE

1. H. E. Ely. "Employment of Negro Man Power in War." *Franklin D. Roosevelt Presidential Library and Museum.* National Archives, 10 Nov. 1925. Web. 22 Jan. 2015.

2. Barry M. Stentiford. *Tuskegee Airmen.* Santa Barbara, CA: ABC-CLIO, 2012. Print. 16.

3. Ibid. 17.

4. Ibid. 18.

5. "Civilian Pilot Training Program." *National Museum of the US Air Force.* National Museum of the US Air Force, 20 Feb. 2015. Web. 13 Apr. 2015.

6. Robert Jakeman. "Tuskegee Flight Training Program." *Encyclopedia of Alabama.* Encyclopedia of Alabama, 31 Mar. 2014. Web. 30 Jan. 2015.

7. Shannon Gary. "Tuskegee University." *Encyclopedia of Alabama.* Encyclopedia of Alabama, 16 June 2014. Web. 14 Apr. 2015.

8. Barry M. Stentiford. *Tuskegee Airmen.* Santa Barbara, CA: ABC-CLIO, 2012. Print. 16.

9. Ibid. 36–37.

10. Ibid.

CHAPTER 5. FROM AFRICA TO EUROPE

1. Barry M. Stentiford. *Tuskegee Airmen.* Santa Barbara, CA: ABC-CLIO, 2012. Print. 51.

2. Leslie O'Flahavan. "African American Pioneers in Aviation." *Smithsonian National Air and Space Museum.* Smithsonian National Air and Space Museum, 1999. Web. 1 Feb. 2015.

3. Marietta Herczeg. "P-40 Warhawk." *Beyond the Band of Brothers.* Beyond the Band of Brothers, 2008. Web. 1 Feb. 2015.

4. Dwight Jon Zimmerman. "Tuskegee Airmen in Operation Corkscrew." *Defense Media Network.* Defense Media Network, 28 May 2013. Web. 13 Apr. 2015.

5. Ibid.

6. Ibid.

SOURCE NOTES
CONTINUED

CHAPTER 6. THE ITALIAN CAMPAIGN

1. "The Italian Campaign." *BBC History*. BBC, 2014. Web. 2 Feb. 2015.

2. Philip L. Bolte and Paul H. Collier. "Italian Campaign." *The War*. PBS, 2007. Web. 14 Apr. 2015.

3. Barry M. Stentiford. *Tuskegee Airmen*. Santa Barbara, CA: ABC-CLIO, 2012. Print. 74–76.

4. Alexander Jefferson with Lewis H. Carlson. *Red Tail Captured, Red Tail Free*. New York: Fordham UP, 2005. Print. 64.

5. "Wings for This Man." *Internet Archive*. Internet Archive, n.d. Web. 13 Apr. 2015.

6. Stephen Sherman. "The Tuskegee Airmen." *Acepilots. com*. Acepilots.com, 29 June 2011. Web. 2 Feb. 2015.

7. Daniel L. Haulman. "112 Victories: Aerial Victory Credits of the Tuskegee Airmen." *Acepilots.com*. Acepilots.com, 31 Mar. 2008. Web. 2 Feb. 2015.

8. Ibid.

CHAPTER 7. THE HOME FRONT

1. Stanley Sandler. *Segregated Skies: All-Black Combat Squadrons of WWII*. Washington, DC: Smithsonian Institution Press, 1992. Print. 82–84.

2. Barry M. Stentiford. *Tuskegee Airmen*. Santa Barbara, CA: ABC-CLIO, 2012. Print. 66.

3. Ibid. 114.

4. Daniel J. Haulman. "Tuskegee Airmen Chronology." *Air Force Historical Research Agency*. Air Force Historical Research Agency, 30 Jan. 2015. Web. 3 Feb. 2015.

CHAPTER 8. POSTWAR CHALLENGES

1. Robert Jablon. "2 Members of Famed World War II Black Flying Squadron, Tuskegee Airmen, Die in US on Same Day." *Fox News.* Fox News, 12 Jan. 2015. Web. 3 Feb. 2015.

2. Keith Rogers. "Tuskegee Airmen Fought War, Segregation." *Las Vegas Review-Journal.* Las Vegas Review-Journal, 4 Aug. 2012. Web. 4 Feb. 2015.

3. Dave Hinton. "After War, Tuskegee Airmen Were Not Allowed to Fly Commercially." *Rantoul Press.* Rantoul Press, 17 Jan. 2012. Web. 4 Feb. 2015.

4. Keith Rogers. "Tuskegee Airmen Fought War, Segregation." *Las Vegas Review-Journal.* Las Vegas Review-Journal, 4 Aug. 2012. Web. 4 Feb. 2015.

5. Ibid.

CHAPTER 9. LEGACY OF THE TUSKEGEE AIRMEN

1. Michael Ray. "Executive Order 9981." *Encyclopaedia Britannica.* Encyclopaedia Britannica, 26 Sept. 2013. Web. 4 Feb. 2015.

2. J. Todd Moye. *Freedom Flyers: The Tuskegee Airmen of World War II.* New York: Oxford UP, 2010. Print. 147.

3. Ibid.

4. Ibid. 146.

5. Ibid.

6. Northwest African American Museum. "Tuskegee Airmen 477th Bombardment Group." *Northwest Connection: The Tuskegee Airmen.* Northwest African American Museum, Sept. 2013. Web. 4 Feb. 2015.

7. Daniel J. Haulman. "Tuskegee Airmen Chronology." *Air Force Historical Research Agency.* Air Force Historical Research Agency, 30 Jan. 2015. Web. 3 Feb. 2015.

8. Keith Rogers. "Tuskegee Airmen Fought War, Segregation." *Las Vegas Review-Journal.* Las Vegas Review-Journal, 4 Aug. 2012. Web. 4 Feb. 2015.

9. Ibid.

10. Katharine Q. Seelye. "Inauguration Is a Culmination for Black Airmen." *New York Times.* New York Times, 9 Dec. 2008. Web. 4 Feb. 2015.

11. "Tuskegee Airmen Congressional Gold Medal." *National Museum of the US Air Force.* National Museum of the US Air Force, 22 Jan. 2015. Web. 13 Apr. 2015.

INDEX

ABOUT THE AUTHOR

Christine Zuchora-Walske has been writing and editing books and articles for children, parents, and teachers for more than 20 years. Her author credits include books for children and young adults on science, history, and current events, books for adults on pregnancy and parenting, and more. Her book *Giant Octopuses* was an IRA Teacher's Choice book for 2001, and *Leaping Grasshoppers* was a 2001 NSTA/CBC Outstanding Science Trade Book for Students. Several of Christine's books have been well-reviewed by *Horn Book* and *School Library Journal*. Christine lives in Minneapolis, Minnesota, with her husband and two children.